NDRAOS · MARIA AQUINO-ALBOR · DONNA ARCANGELI · GEORGE ATALLAH · SYLVIA ATENCIA · PAMELA AURORA · SUSAN BABINECK
BO · CINDY BARNES · KIM BARNETT · STACY BARNETT · WIMBERLY BARRA · BRUCE BARTON · FRANCES BARTON · KEVIN BATCHELOR
ORY BENJAMIN · TAMMIE BENSON · ALICIA BERG · CASSANDRA BERRY · CATHY BERRYHILL · CAT
CKIE BOYD · AUDNA BRADY · LINETTE BRITO · ARLIS BRODIE · JOHN BROOKBY · DARIN BROOKS
NTHIA CARPENTER · BETSY CASTRO · MARK CENTORE · CARON CHATHAM · SLAYDEN CLARKSO
WFORD · CARL CROSS · ANDRES CUETO · KENNETH CVEJANOVICH · SUSAN DALEY-FALLON · KEITH DALHOVER · MARKO DASIGENIS
SUSAN DIETERICH · SERGIO DIGIORGIO · JENNIFER DILL · TERRI DINGLE · CARLO DINUNZIO · CHAI-LEONG DIONG · KELLEY DIXO
CHIK · STEPHEN DUNHAM · DANIELLE DUNN · KIM DUTKOSKY · ASHLEIGH EDMUNDSON · STEVEN EDWARDS · ANITA ECKHARDT
H FARRIS · RAFAEL FEINSTEIN · GRANT FISHER · DAVID FLICKINGER · WULF FOCKE · SHAWNA FORBES · JOSEPH FOSTER · PETER FOXLEY
OVIC · ROCIO GALINDO · MINERVA GARCIA · JOHN GARLAND · JULIE GARZA · LEANNA GATLIN · ANN GATTON · GRANT GEHRING
CAMERON GOLDSMITH · LAURA GONZALES · RACHEL GONZALES · ALBERTO GONZALEZ · JOSE GONZALEZ · YVETTE GONZALEZ
NNELLS · GEORGINA GUZMAN · FAEZEH HAKIMZADEH · ALAN HALEY · JENNIFER HALL-DUDLEY · CHARLES HAMEL · JAMES HANLIN
MARK HELM · MICHAEL HENDERSHOT · ELYSE HERMAN · HECTOR HERNANDEZ · HOMER HERNANDEZ · NICOLE HERNANDEZ-BARRIOS
HO · TAYLOR HOHERTZ · LUCY HOLMES · KATIE HONEYCUTT · RACHEL HOOVER · ROBERT HOOVER · EVAN HOPKINS · COLLEEN HOPPER
RWIN · CAROL JACKSON · YRONDA JACKSON-SPURS · CHARLES JACOBS · SAMANTHA JANDER · ALLISON JANSON · AMY JOCHEM
STL · HAYTHAM KADER · RHONDA KAISER · MOLLY KALLIENY · KRISTI KANGAS · JOHN KAUFMAN · LESLIE KAYLE · STEPHANIE KAUP
VELL · JEANNE KING · MICHELLE KING · ALICE KITTLER · ANNA KLAPPENBACH · MICHAELA KNIGHT · ANDREW KOPY · ERIC KORTH
KUTTLER · ALEJANDRO LAGO · ANASTASIA LALLAS · ELLEN LANG · LISA LAU · SAMSON LAUON · LOAN LE · DIANE LEATHERWOOD
NG-MIN LIN · YANG LIU · STEPHANIE LIVELY · LOTUS LOCASTE · PAUL LODHOLZ · MARCO LOPEZ · TAMI LOVE · CONRAD LOZANO
KATHERINE MARQUEZ · CLAIRE MARTIN · TODD MARTIN · JOHN MASON · ANGELA MAYER · SANDRA MAYFIELD · PATRICIA MCBRAYER
MCGLONE · DALLAS MCINGVALE · MOLLY MCINTYRE-HAIR · KATE MCMILLAN · CHERYL MELTON · OMAR MENDIOLA · KEITH MESSICK
E · MAHBUBA MOKIM · DONN MOLL · GUSTAVO MONTIEL · MIRTHA MORALES · RAFAEL MORALES · RENE MORAN · JACLYN MORFIN
AGHDALI · JOSEPH NASH · MANUEL NAVARRO · CHAD NEAL · MATTHEW NGO · CHRISTINE NGUYEN · KIMYEN NGUYEN · MY NGUYEN
ENS · DAVID PAINTER · JESSIE PALACIOS · ANDREW PALMER · MICHAEL PAMATMAT · JUSTUS PANG · KAREN PANICO · MINSIK PARK
REZ · CHRIS PETRASH · TRINH PHAM · TUNG PHAM · JULIANA PINTO · JOHN PITRE · DAN POEHLER · EDUARDO PONCE DE LEON
ARLENE RATY · ADAN RAZO · CAROLINE REES · TESS REGAN · CAROLYN REGGINS · ROBERT REID · CHELSEA REIMER · REBECCA REYNA
IGUEZ · YVONNE RODRIGUEZ · BERNARD ROGERS · JANET ROGERS · SARAH RONAN · ROSALIE ROSS · WILL ROSS · PATRICIA ROUNTREE
Z · JAMAL SALEM · VERONICA SANTIAGO · DEBRA SAPPINGTON · RHEA ANN SAWYER · JULIA SCHAFER · VIANA SCHARUNOVYCH
RY SEWAL · SAMANTHA SEYLER · LYNNE SHAFER · KATHERINE SHANNON · ANDREW SHEEHAN · SHERYL SHELLENE · TANIKA SHIRLEY
PAUL SMEAD · MELINDA SMILJANIC · CAROLINE SMITH · LEWIS SMITH · MARTHA SMITH · WILLIAM SMITH · KARENE SMITHHART
FFREY STAIT · STEPHEN STARENSIER · JONATHAN STURT · IVAN SUE · JAMES SULLIVAN · LISA SURPRENANT · KIMBERLY TAMBORELLO
ORRES · DANA TRAMMEL · AUBREY TUCKER · ADRIENNE TURNER · CRAIG UPTMOR · SANDRA VACCARI · JOHN VALDEZ · MIA VALE
ERRETT · SCOTT VICKNAIR · RICHARD VICKREY · ALMA VILLANUEVA · AMY VO · KELLY VOEHRINGER · MAE WADE · SHELBY WALKER
LY WERTZ · JONATHAN WEST · WENDY WESTFAUL · SARA WHITEHEAD · PAUL WILKINSON · TARA WILLIAMS · CATHERINE WILLIAMS-COBB
NTERS · KATE WOMACK · SEONGHYEAK WON · BLAKE WOODS · WENDY WRIGHT · JULIANA YOUNG · MARY ANN YOUNG · BIN YU
NIEL ZERMENO · ANISSA ZICKLER · MARY KATHERINE ZIEGLER · SCOTT ZIEGLER · SANJA ZILIC · FRANK ZISTLER · ALBERTO ZUNIGA

# ZIEGLER COOPER

**40 YEARS** OF INSPIRATIONAL DESIGN

Visual Profile Books, New York

Pictured: Founding principals Scott Ziegler (left) and Michael Cooper (right).

# INTRODUCTION

## A FIRM WHOSE TIME HAS COME

Some individuals know early in life that they are destined to be architects. Others come to architecture in due course, which is the path that brought Scott Ziegler, AIA and Michael Cooper, AIA together in a master's program at Rice University School of Architecture. Neither Ziegler nor Cooper had any previous background in architecture before arriving at Rice, but both were eager and passionate to become architects. Ziegler came with a bachelor's degree in business administration, and Cooper came with a bachelor's degree in economics. Being gutsy entrepreneurs determined to succeed in their newly chosen field, Ziegler and Cooper decided to open their own firm before graduation. And so they did, in 1977, leveraging their combined degrees and graduate studies.

Of course, every fledgling practice takes time to mature. Ziegler and Cooper would never forget their early lesson in business risk management. While still at Rice, the two classmates pioneered a dual role of architect/developer to design and build urban lofts for their very first project. As fate would have it, a homeless person started a fire that completely destroyed the entire project. Fortunately, most milestones in the growth of the firm produced much happier outcomes as it learned to create superior buildings for clients, master new technologies and methodologies, and cultivate the expertise, skills and contacts to secure major commissions.

## A VISION OF DESIGN

Since its founding, Ziegler Cooper has been guided by a strong belief that beautiful architecture enriches people's lives, uplifts the human spirit, and provides a constant vision of excellence. Its faith in the power of design fueled its success. To support its belief, the firm established specialized internal studios that serve mankind's most basic needs to live, learn, work and worship, assigning a principal of the firm to lead each studio. By organizing early into dedicated studios, Ziegler Cooper gave its staff the means to develop specialized practice areas, and to build a knowledge base to serve the needs of its clients. At the same time, the firm declared its commitment to the design of specific building types, assuring clients with particular needs that their projects would be handled well no matter how demanding they might be.

Today, Ziegler Cooper is a respected, award-winning architecture practice with a solid client base and projects that stretch from coast to coast. The firm has gained prominence for its creative response to the growing demand for urban living, the evolution of the workplace, and the contemporary needs of religious, institutional and community organizations. Its body of work includes commercial office buildings, corporate campuses, interior architecture, high-rise and mid-rise residential towers, hotels, retail, churches, schools and community buildings.

An analysis of the firm's body of work identifies recurring design themes that can be characterized as crisp, modern expressions of a building's form. They are inspired by organic and natural forms, utilizing texture, color and materiality as the medium to capture the interplay of light and space. Each of the firm's designs begins with a site strategy that is clearly organized and represents the client's program. In the firm's search for an appropriate solution, there is a constant dialogue between interior and exterior spaces to engage the building with its context and its surroundings. As the design becomes three-dimensional, harmony and proportion are expressed in the composition of the building's plan, sections and elevations. To design beautiful buildings, Ziegler Cooper has learned that an architect's best friends are his convictions, perseverance, and patience.

## THE FORMATIVE YEARS

Ziegler Cooper's 1980 founding of the Houston Architectural Laboratory (HAL), a CAD workshop that predated AutoCAD, was based on the partners' conviction that desktop computing had a promising future as a forerunner in the database management of design, construction and real estate. By creating a digital database of building documentation, the firm provided building owners and managers a means to digitally verify and validate leasable space. This greatly improved building management and leasing tool created a valuable entrée for the young firm to the world of commercial and corporate real estate clients.

The closing of the Houston office of design giant Skidmore, Owings & Merrill represented a strategic growth opportunity for Ziegler Cooper in 1988. Seizing the opportunity, Ziegler Cooper hired key design professionals – a huge financial risk for the young firm – in a strategy that proved to be a transformational investment. Adding Louis Skidmore, Jr. as a partner bolstered the firm's ability to enter the elite ranks of high-rise building architects, and elevated the public's perception of the firm's capabilities.

## HIGHER ASPIRATIONS

Having designed its first high-rise building for BMC Software's headquarters in 1994, Ziegler Cooper followed up with several high-rise residential buildings that created a solid foundation for its work in urban residential architecture. In 2000, the firm's outlook changed dramatically when the Archdiocese of Galveston Houston selected Ziegler Cooper as the architect for the Co-Cathedral of the Sacred Heart in Houston. Not only does a cathedral hold vast spiritual significance for a community, this particular Catholic cathedral would be the first built anywhere in the United States for more than half a century. The project award lifted the firm's aspirations to a new level, fulfilling Archbishop Fiorenza's wish that the cathedral be an inspiration for the ages via an expression of "noble simplicity." Visits

to European cathedrals by the design team revealed how a magnificent interplay of light and space could express an ethereal, spiritual quality. The Co-Cathedral design perfectly captures all of these qualities and has become an important Houston landmark.

At one point, the project's budget was questioned, and an aesthetic dispute arose when the Archbishop sought to lower the height of the building to save money. Ziegler Cooper defended its work in terms of the timeless principles of cathedral architecture rather than resorting to building economics. "I invoked Palladio's concepts for ideal building proportions and the important interplay of divine light on the sacred space, then brazenly compared the Archbishop's cost saving suggestion to Medici's asking Michelangelo to shorten the marble statue of David by cutting away his mid-section to save a few Lira!" Ziegler remembers. "Thankfully, the Archbishop accepted my explanation, and hailed the final design as 'a Great Cathedral for a Great City.'"

## GIVING YOUR BEST

Four decades after its founding, Ziegler Cooper is clearly a firm on the rise, with the commissions, clients and accolades that accrue to professionals who know what they are doing and enjoy contributing to the good of individuals, organizations and society. Every thriving architecture practice has its own reasons for success. At Ziegler Cooper, it is the firm's passionate pursuit of beauty, and its mastery of the aesthetic, technical and economic issues associated with good design that is striking and timely.

Given the firm's early focus on urban infill projects, it is not surprising to find that an enduring passion for urban design continues to motivate the firm. "With the population migrating back to more dense urban areas," Ziegler comments, "we find our future bright, as we reshape the landscape of the markets we serve and breathe new life into new urban districts. We're working where young Americans want to be, trying to balance the demands of the 24/7 lifestyle and create more livable cities." Under Ziegler's leadership, the Urban Residential Studio has master planned, designed and constructed high-rise condominiums, hotels, lofts and high-rise apartments totaling over 22 million square feet to date, all across the nation.

The Commercial Office and Corporate Facility Studio, led by Kurt Hull, AIA, LEED AP, who has managed some of the firm's largest, most complex projects, has been cited as a cutting edge design studio and thought leader for corporate office parks and build-to-suit projects. The studio is responsible for nearly 20 million square feet of corporate and commercial office buildings, nearly a half billion square feet of master planning and mixed use projects, and five million square feet of commercial redevelopment. The studio is recognized as expert in formulating performance-driven buildings that fulfill the needs of owners, occupants, and investors.

The Workplace Interiors Studio at Ziegler Cooper has built a strong recognition in the workplace market for specialized design expertise of energy companies, financial services, banking, law firms, consulting, insurance, engineering companies, and creative office space. Led by Mark Nolen, AIA, LEED AP, Ziegler Cooper serves as architect of record for more than 100 office buildings, with 50 million square feet of tenant space.

The firm's work with institutional clients has been equally impressive. The Worship, Educational and Community Studio, led by Stephen Lucchesi, AIA, has brought together talent and expertise that is currently at work on 30 campuses in a variety of community based projects. Besides having the requisite professional qualifications, the studio is adept at building the close working relationships required by institutional clients. Planning a place of worship is one of the most challenging and rewarding experiences a congregation will undertake. As the studio is well aware, the design of

worship spaces becomes an outward expression of faith and a physical invitation for others to join in the celebration of worship.

## THE YEARS AHEAD

Ziegler Cooper faces the future with an undiminished appetite for fresh challenges and demanding assignments. Yet the firm has also decided not to be all things to all people. "We enjoy keeping in close contact with the communities we serve. Even though technology has changed the way we practice, we still embrace the physical nature of architecture, the people, and the locations in which we work. While we respect large, global firms, we don't want to be one ourselves," Ziegler admits. After three successful acquisitions, including the most recent merger of HBL into the community architecture studio, the firm will continue to look for similar opportunities as it nurtures internal growth.

The belief that the densification and urbanization of large U.S. cities is a vital, sustainable urban growth strategy remains an enduring vision for Ziegler Cooper. "We enjoy design on an urban scale to create a distinct sense of place and enhance the sense of community," Ziegler says. "As a result, our work plays a significant role in who we are and who we want to become."

History has taught us that a city's greatness is measured in large part by the quality of its art, architecture and urban environment. Yet many urban communities around the country have yet to realize but a fraction of their potential. Seeing an enormous opportunity in meeting this challenge, Ziegler Cooper is prepared to show what it can do.

R. Scott Ziegler, AIA
Founding Principal | Principal-In-Charge, Urban Residential Studio

# 40

**Years in Houston: Key Firm Milestones**

| 1973-76 | 1977 | 1980 | 1982 | 1983 | 1987 | 1988 | 1992 |

**1973-76**
Scott Ziegler and Michael Cooper met in Masters program at Rice University.

**1977**
Ziegler Cooper founded by Scott Ziegler and Michael Cooper.

**1980**
Kurt Hull joins the firm.

**1982**
Formation of Houston Architectural Lab (HAL) to graphically document 30 million SF of base buildings throughout all 50 states.

**1983**
Mark Nolen joins the firm.

**1987**
Firm Celebrates 10th Anniversary with over 30 employees.

**1988**
SOM closes doors to Houston office and Ziegler Cooper makes strategic decision to incorporate key players from SOM, including Louis Skidmore, Jr. Firm reorganizes into LIVE, LEARN, WORK & WORSHIP Place Studios.

**1992**
Construction completes for TEPPCO Headquarters and Space Industries.

| 2001 | 2002 | 2004 | 2005 | 2006 | 2007 | 2008 |

**2001**
Completion of University of St. Thomas Malloy Hall, the last building on Phillip Johnson's master plan.

**2002**
Completion of Alley Theatre Center for Production.

**2004**
Completion of The Kinkaid School Center for Student Life, Fine Arts & Academic Building.

**2005**
Firm wins design competition for design of The Austonian, which becomes Austin's tallest building.

**2006**
Completion of St. John's School additions and renovations.

**2007**
Firm celebrates 30th Anniversary party at Co-Cathedral of the Sacred Heart with 75 employees and reaches $15.7 Million in revenue.

**2008**
The Co-Cathedral of the Sacred Heart is dedicated and Paul Lodholz joins the firm as Principal-in-Charge of the Worship Place Studio.

**1993**

Firm Completes BMC Software and Houston Industries.

**1994**

Construction completes for Allen Center architectural redevelopment.

**1996**

Construction completes for Louisiana Place architectural redevelopment.

**1997**

Firm celebrates 20th Anniversary with 60 employees and reaches $4.9 Million in revenue.

**1999**

America Tower commercial redevelopment completes and firm reaches $10.5 Million in revenue.

**2000**

Construction completes on Villa d'Este, the firms first residential high-rise tower. Montebello project kicks off at sister property, and is later featured in *Architectural Digest.*

**2000**

Ziegler Cooper commissioned to design the Co-Cathedral of the Sacred Heart. Received call from Archbishop Joseph Fiorenza on All Saints Day.

**2009**

Construction completes for 2727 Kirby and firm is awarded its first "Mega Church" project, a 2,500-seat worship center and 500-seat chapel for First Baptist Pasadena.

**2010**

Ziegler Cooper and Odell Associates form ZC+O, a strategic alliance to land Research Forest Lakeside which includes master planning and design services for a 76-acre, mixed-use office park totalling over 1,798,398 sf.

**2013**

Firm hits record revenue of $21.6 Million and employs over 96 employees. Firm designs and moves into new offices at Bank of America Center, which receives LEED Gold.

**2014**

Construction completes at The Sovereign at Regent Square. Ziegler Cooper's Urban Residential Studio is responsible for half of the residential units on the boards or under construction in Houston's Central Business District.

**2015**

The Worship & Education Studio of Ziegler Cooper merges with HBL Architects to form the Worship, Education and Community Studio under Principal-in-Charge Stephen Lucchesi, AIA.

**2017**

Firm celebrates 40th anniversary with more than 100 employees and an urban residential portfolio totaling over $4.4 billion.

# CONTENTS

15

16

Preston Hollow Village
**Dallas, Texas | 2017**

20

24

Aris Market Square
**Houston, Texas | 2017**

30

2727 Kirby
**Houston, Texas | 2009**

37

The Sovereign

**Houston, Texas | 2014**

Gables Park Tower
**Austin, Texas | 2013**

48

One Lake's Edge at Hughes Landing

**The Woodlands, Texas | 2015**

Hughes Landing Apartment Tower
**The Woodlands, Texas | 2019**

Gables Cherry Creek
**Denver, Colorado | 2016**

GABLES JACKSON

Hines Sloans Lake
**Denver, Colorado | 2018**

75

Dinerstein 7th & Grant
Denver, Colorado | 2018

Gables River Oaks
**Houston, Texas | 2013**

83

Villa d'Este & Montebello

**Houston, Texas | 2001**

86

Gables Westcreek

**Houston, Texas | 2019**

95

Block 98

**Houston, Texas | 2019**

Olympia at Willowick Park
**Houston, Texas | 2015**

Highland Tower
**Houston, Texas | 2011**

The Broadway
**San Antonio, Texas | 2010**

113

The Sapphire
**South Padre Island, Texas | 2006**

Barryknoll
**Houston, Texas | 2018**

118

121

The Midtown
**Houston, Texas | 2019**

122

125

Avant Buffalo Bayou
**Houston, Texas | 2019**

Avant Post Oak Park
**Houston, Texas | 2019**

132

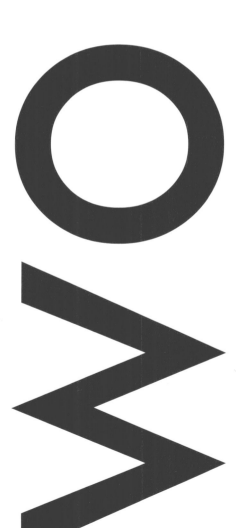

work

Research Forest Lakeside 4 & 5

**The Woodlands, Texas | 2014**

143

147

152

Dress For Success
**Houston, Texas | 2012**

Chicago Bridge & Iron
**The Woodlands, Texas | 2015**

163

Confidential Office Tower

**Austin, Texas | 2018**

169

Research Forest Lakeside 2

**The Woodlands, Texas | 2011**

Westchase Park II
Houston, Texas | 2015

174

179

800 Bell

**Houston, Texas | 2017**

182

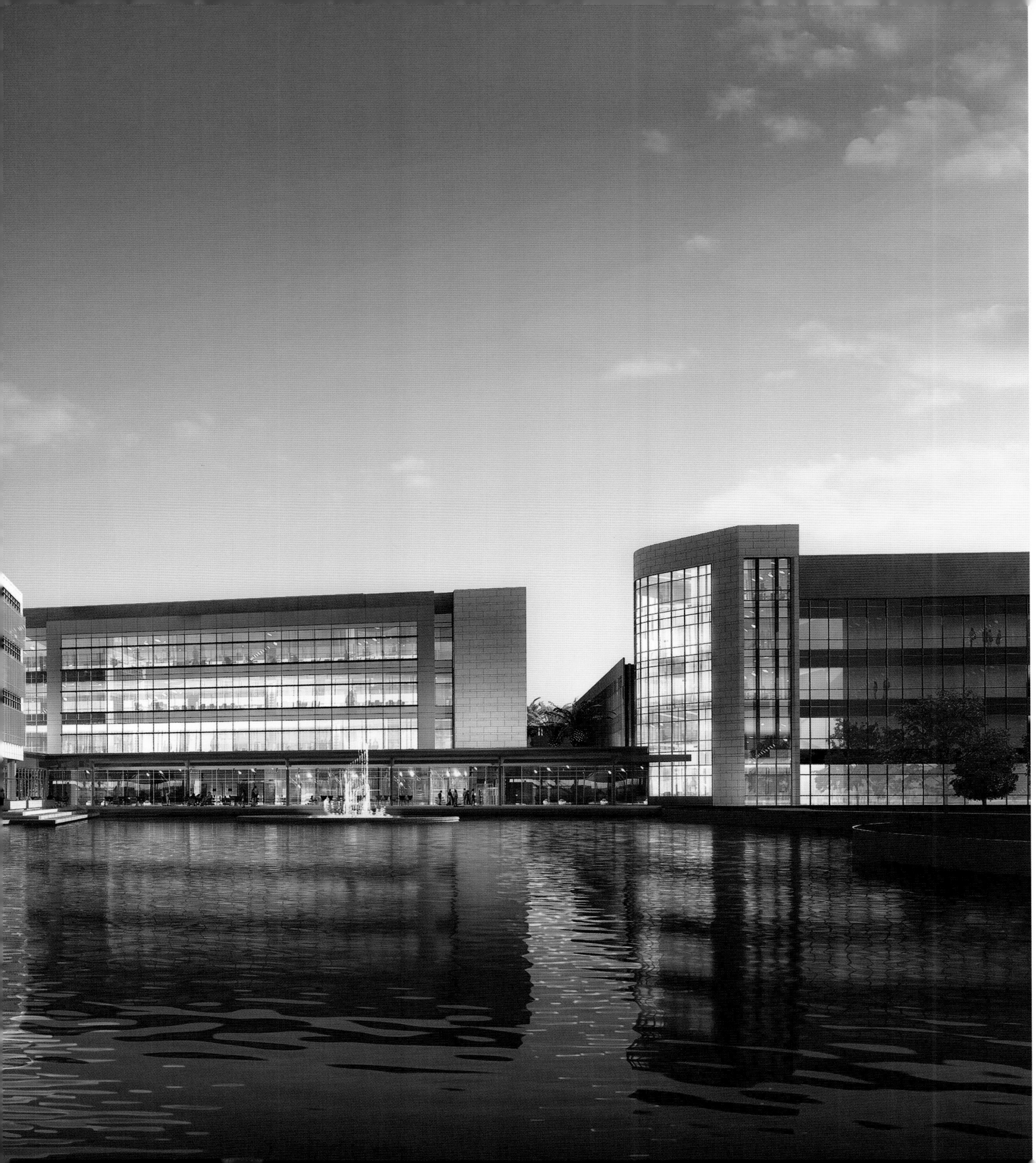

Confidential Corporate Campus

**Houston, Texas | 2013**

190

Woodlands Gate

**Houston, Texas | 2018**

201

Tempe Mixed-Use Development
**Tempe, Arizona | 2016**

207

*Morgan Smith Street*
**Houston, Texas | 2018**

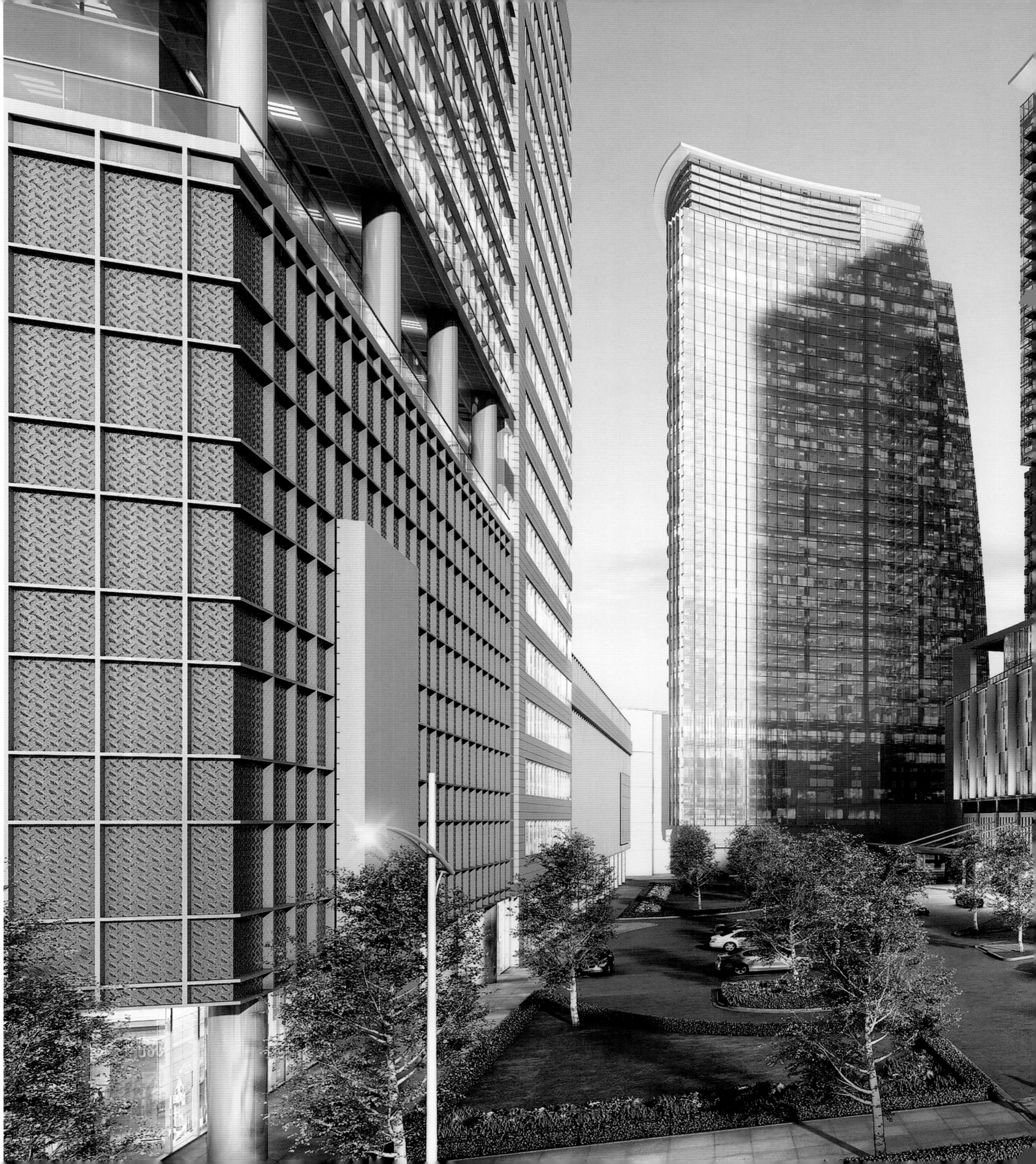

The Perennial
**Houston, Texas | 2016**

G.E. Turtle Creek

**Dallas, Texas | 2014**

220

PMRG Hotel & Residences

**Houston, Texas | 2019**

EASTSHORE RETAIL CENTER

RESTAURANT

RETAIL

innovate

232

235

G&A Partners

**Houston, Texas | 2016**

Parkway Properties
**Houston, Texas | 2016**

Repsol
**The Woodlands, Texas | 2014**

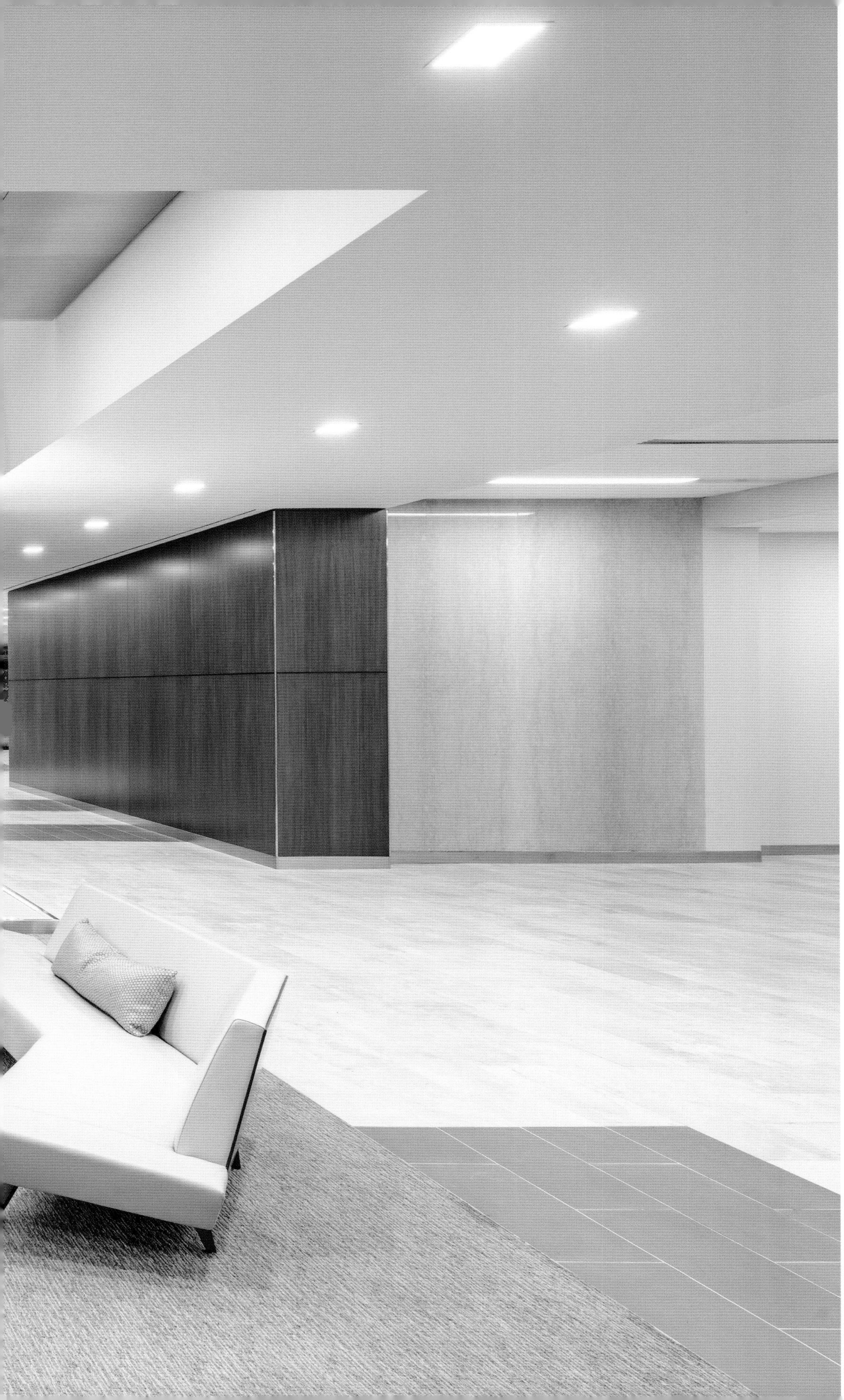

3 Greenway

**Houston, Texas | 2016**

20 Greenway

**Houston, Texas | 2015**

Apache Corporation
**Houston, Texas | 2015**

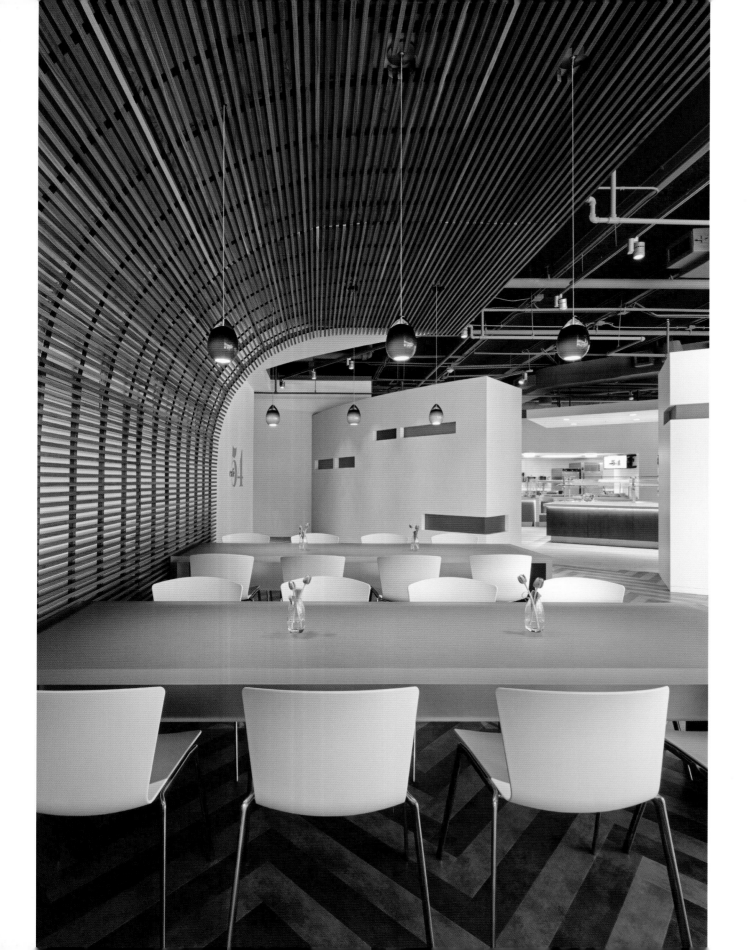

266

Alliantgroup
**Houston, Texas | 2014**

271

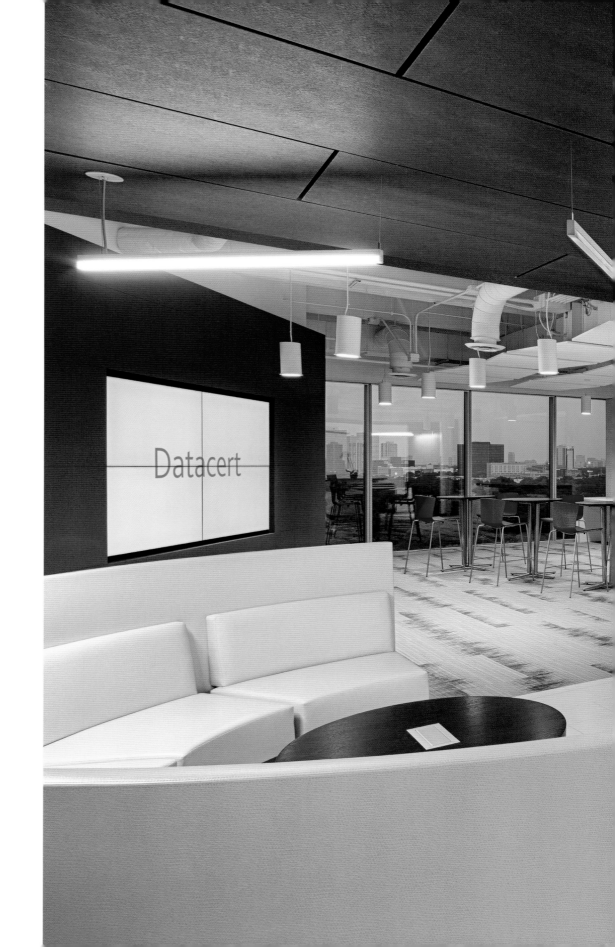

Datacert

**Houston, Texas | 2015**

Parker Drilling
**Houston, Texas | 2008**

Stoller Group

Houston, Texas | 2016

W.D. Von Gonten

**Houston, Texas | 2016**

Skanska
**Houston, Texas | 2015**

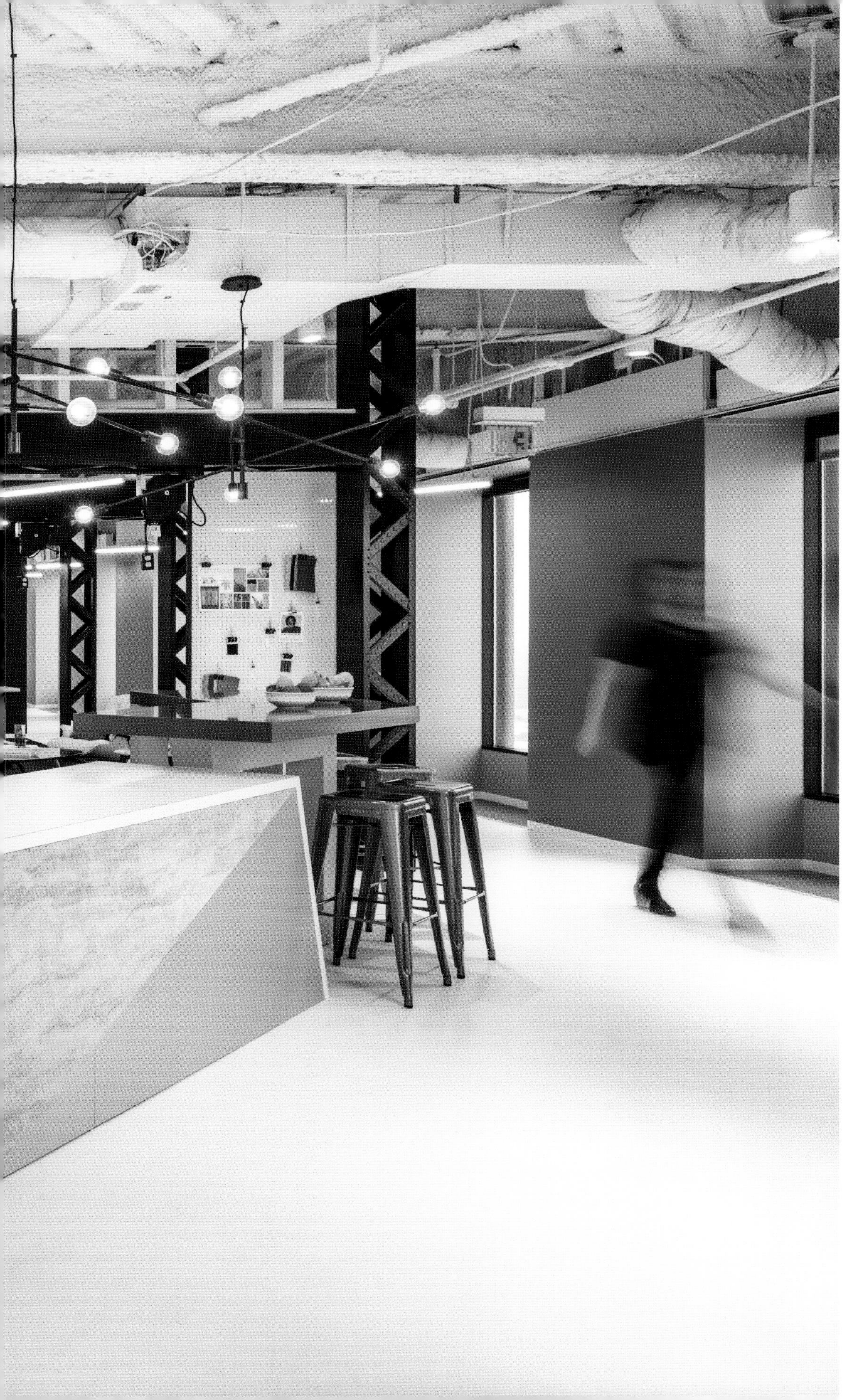

DesignHive

**Houston, Texas | 2017**

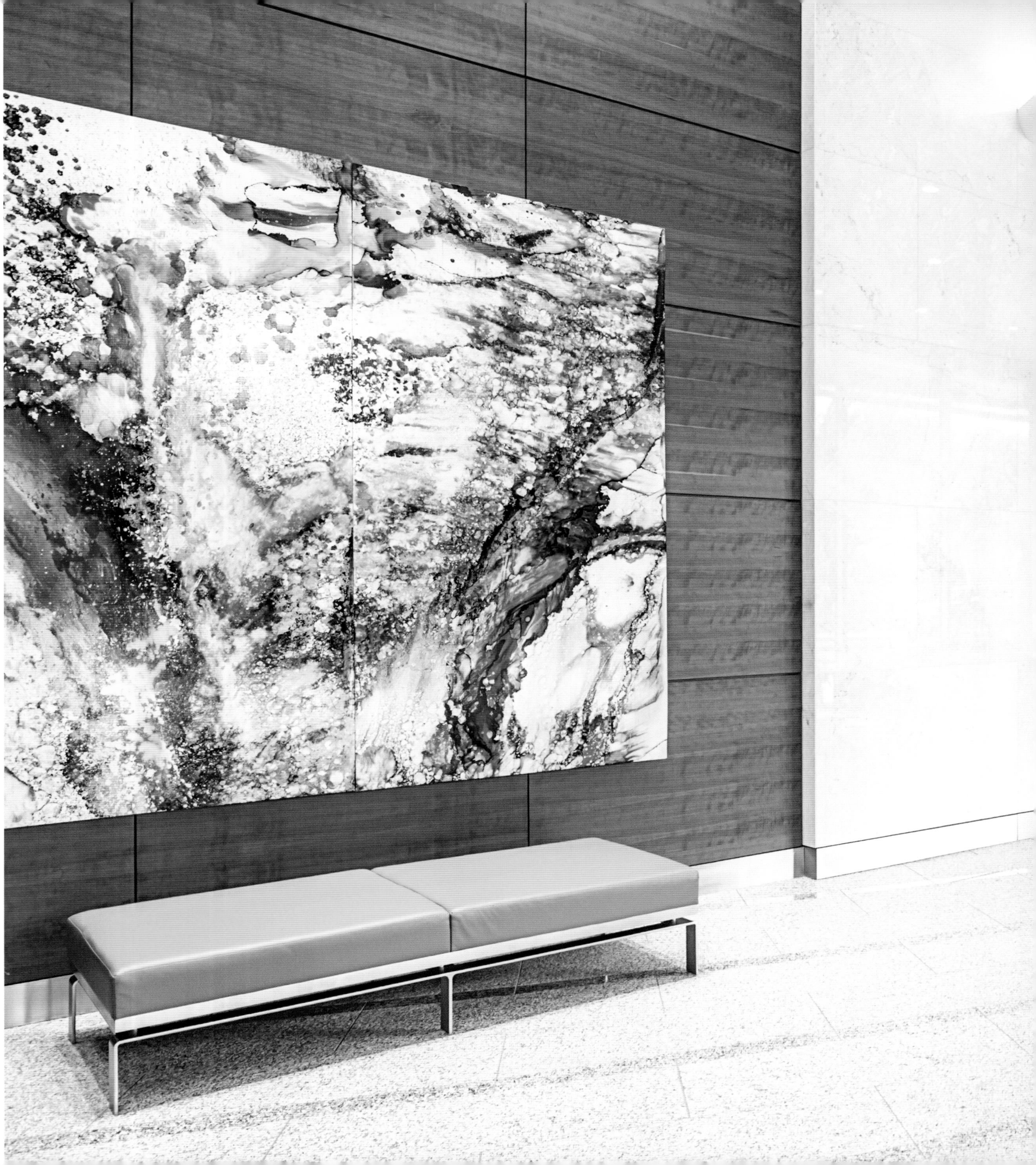

Four Oaks
**Houston, Texas | 2016**

303

worship

Co-Cathedral of the Sacred Heart
**Houston, Texas | 2008**

306

Kingwood United Methodist Church

**Kingwood, Texas | 2015**

Memorial Lutheran Church and School
**Houston, Texas | 2010**

First Baptist Church Pasadena

**Pasadena, Texas | 2012**

324

St. John Lutheran Church and School
**Cypress, Texas | 2011**

Universal Church Westpark

**Houston, Texas | 2012**

336

Sacred Heart Catholic Church

**Conroe, Texas | 2016**

341

Christ Church United Methodist

**The Woodlands, Texas | 2011**

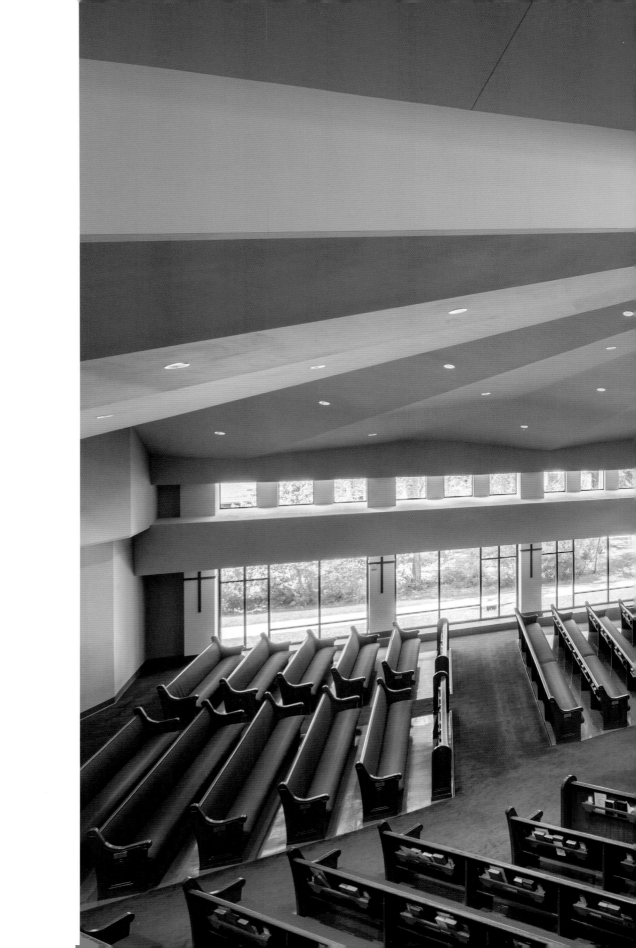

348

The John Cooper School
**The Woodlands, Texas | 2016**

353

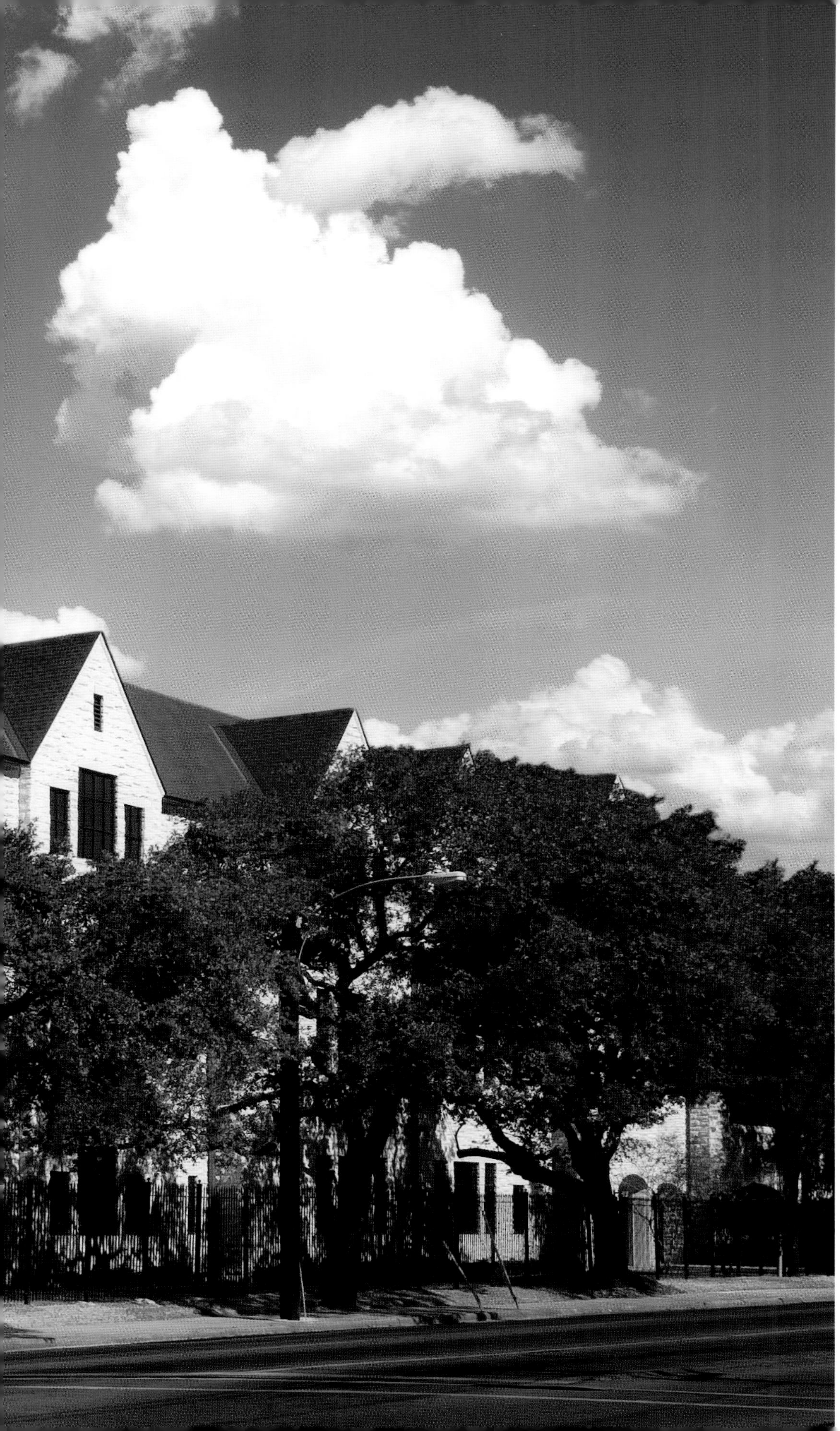

St. John School
**Houston, Texas | 2007**

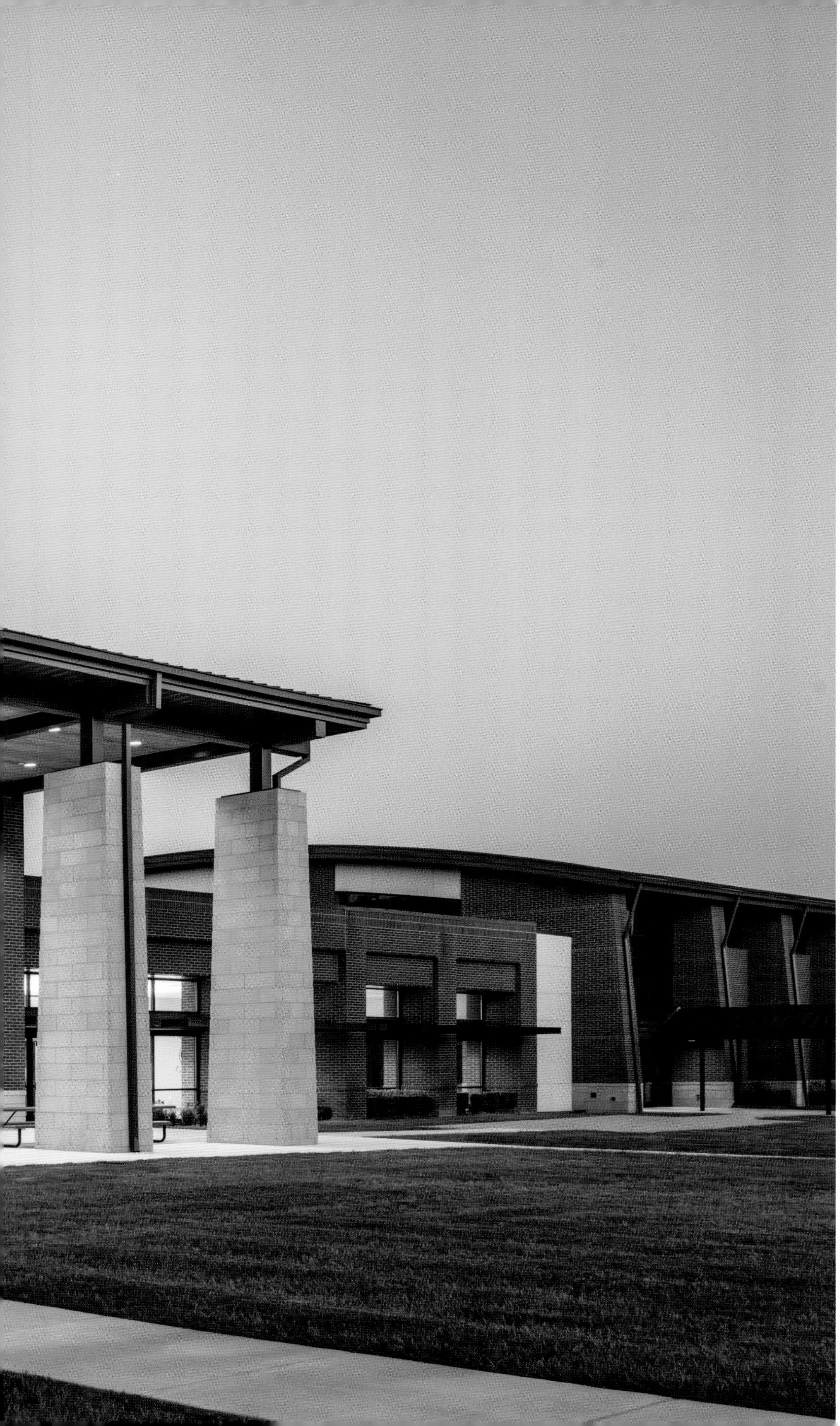

Pope John XXIII High School

**Katy, Texas | 2015**

The Village School

**Houston, Texas | 2015**

371

St. Rose of Lima Catholic School
**Houston, Texas | 2012**

379

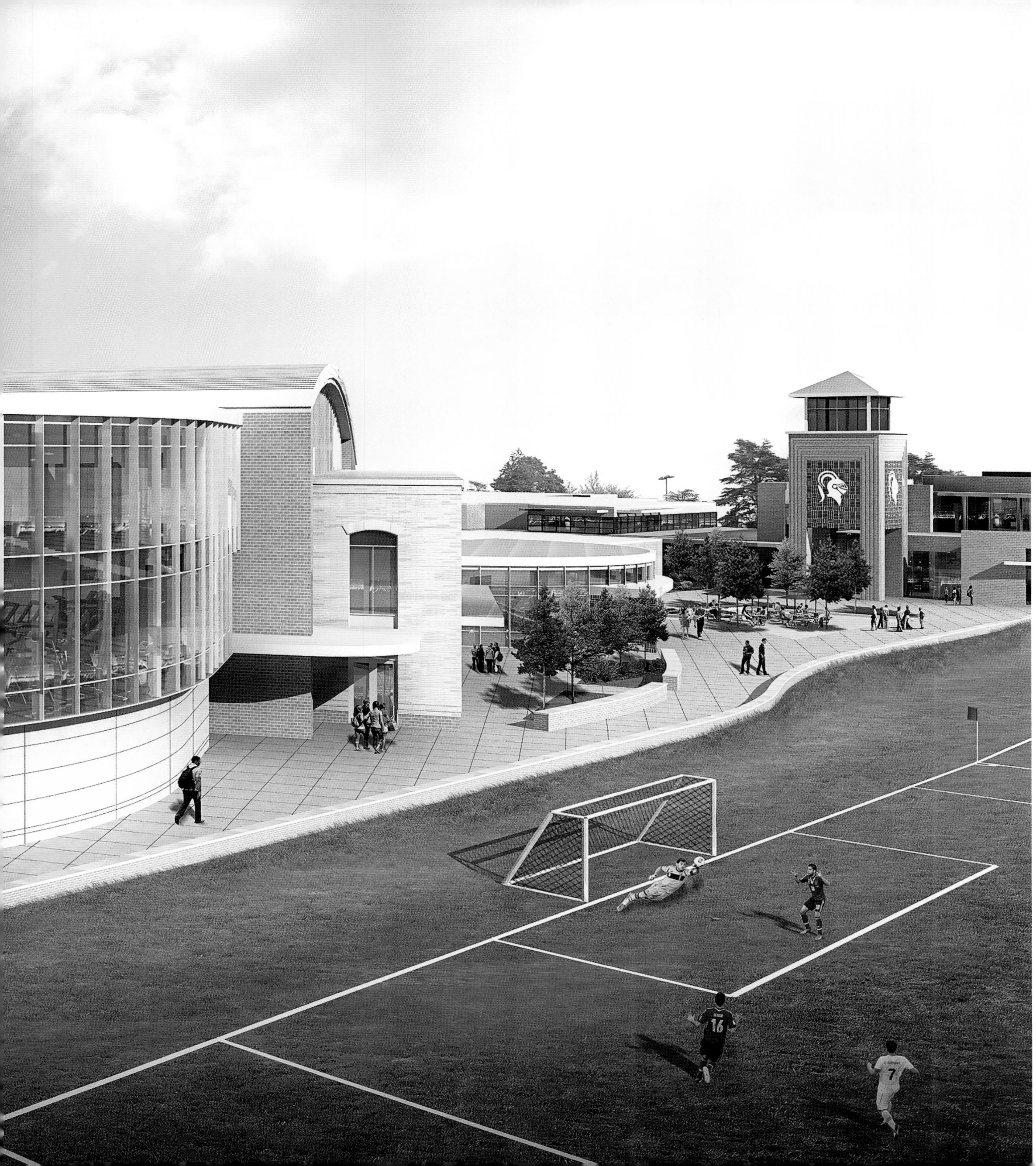

Episcopal High School

**Houston, Texas | 2017**

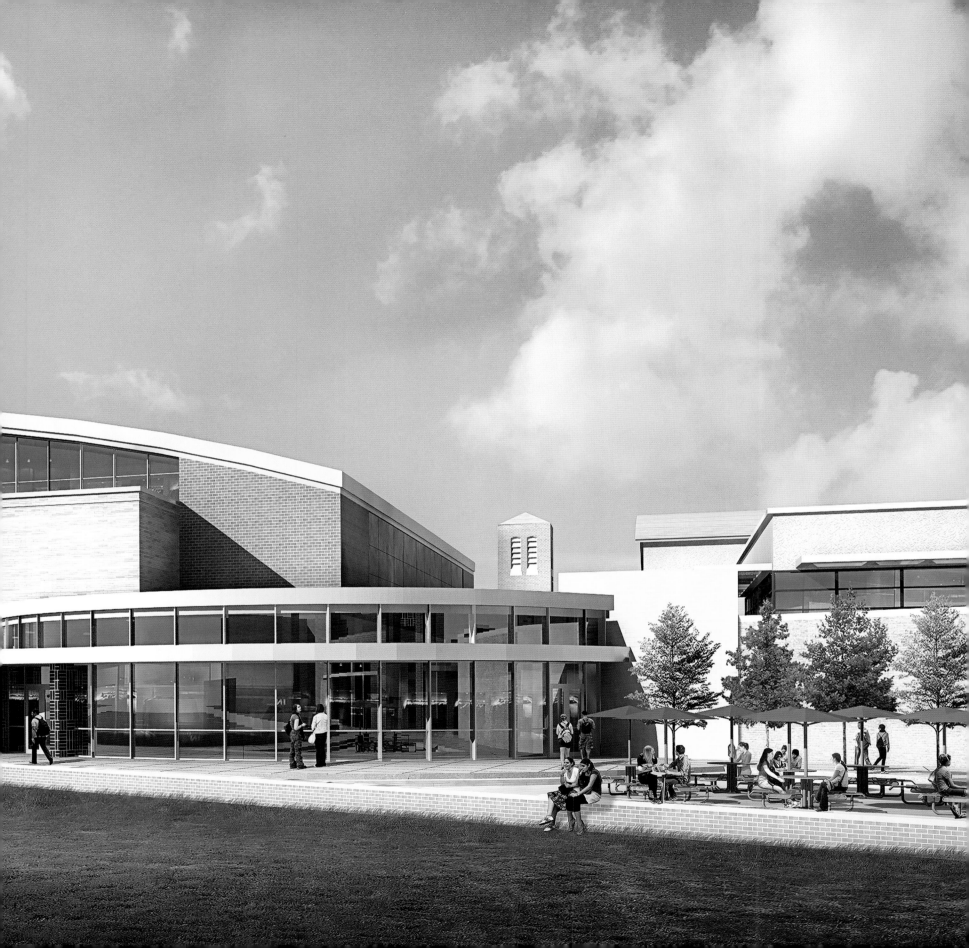

# projects

**Bolsover Street Residences**
2 Townhouses
Houston, Texas
1979

**Skilling Residence**
Houston, Texas
1980

**Skilling Residence**
Utopia, Texas
1980

**Ziegler Lodge**
Log Home
Snowmass, Colorado
1988

**Ziegler Nautical Cottage**
Kemah, Texas
1988

**Tallichet House**
Kemah, Texas
1990

**Ziegler Residence Ella Lee Lane**
Houston, Texas
1990

**Sprague Residence**
Kemah, Texas
2001

**TCYC Club House**
Kemah, Texas
2010

**URBAN RESIDENTIAL HIGH-RISES**

**Villa d'Este Residences**
28-Story Tower
Houston, Texas
1999

**Montebello Residences**
30-Story Tower
Houston, Texas
2001

**The Sapphire Residences**
30-Story Tower
South Padre Island, Texas
2006

**2727 Kirby Residences**
28-Story Tower
Houston, Texas
2009

**The Austonian Residences & Retail**
56-Story Tower
Austin, Texas
2009

**The Broadway Residences**
21-Story Tower
San Antonio, Texas
2010

**Highland Tower Residences**
16-Story Tower
Houston, Texas
2011

**Gables Park Tower Apartments**
18-Story Tower
Austin, Texas
2013

**The Sovereign Apartments**
21-Story Tower
Houston, Texas
2014

**West Village Forest City Residences**
21-Story Tower
Dallas, Texas
2014

**Light Street Apartments**
30-Story Tower
Baltimore, Maryland
2015

**Hanover Southampton Apartments**
12-Story Tower
Houston, Texas
2016

**Gables Uptown Apartments & Retail**
28-Story Tower
Houston, Texas
2016

**Hines Aris Market Square Apartments**
32-Story Tower
Houston, Texas
2017

**Marquette Catalyst Apartments & Retail**
28-Story Tower
Houston, Texas
2017

**Southern Land Apartments**
13-Story Tower
Las Vegas, Nevada
2017

**Greystar Parq on Speer Apartments**
18-Story Tower
Denver, Colorado
2018

**Gables Jackson Apartments**
12-Story Tower
Denver, Colorado
2018

**Camden Conte Apartments**
21-Story Tower
Houston, Texas
2019

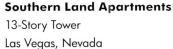

**Caydon Midtown
Apartments**
27-Story Tower
Houston, Texas
2019

**Trammell Crow Block 98
Apartments**
34-Story Tower
Houston, Texas
2019

**Gables Westcreek Apartments**
15-Story Tower
Houston, Texas
2019

**Avant Buffalo Bayou
Apartments**
30-Story Tower
Houston, Texas
2019

**Avant Post Oak Park
Apartments**
30-Story Tower
Houston, Texas
2019

**Hughes Landing Apartment Tower**
23-Story Tower
The Woodlands, Texas
2019

**JLB Buckhead Apartments
& Retail**
13-Story Tower
Atlanta, Georgia
2019

**The Driscoll Apartments
& Retail**
30-Story Tower
Houston, Texas
2019

**URBAN RESIDENTIAL MID-RISES**

**Waterway Lofts One**
6-Story Mid-rise
The Woodlands, Texas
2003

**The Empire Residences**
8-Story Mid-rise
Houston, Texas
2005

**Waterway Lofts Two**
7-Story Mid-rise
The Woodlands, Texas
2005

**The Briarglen Residences**
8-Story Mid-rise
Houston, Texas
2006

**Gables Memorial Hills Apartments**
8-Story Mid-rise
Houston, Texas
2009

**Gables Park Plaza One Apartments**
8-Story Mid-rise
Austin, Texas
2009

**Gables Tanglewood
Apartments & Retail**
8-Story Mid-rise
Houston, Texas
2013

**Gables River Oaks Apartments**
8-Story Mid-rise
Houston, Texas
2013

**Morgan City Center Apartments**
8-Story Mid-rise
Houston, Texas
2014

**Archstone Kirby Apartments**
8-Story Mid-rise
Houston, Texas
2014

**Millennium Rainey Street Apartments**
8-Story Mid-rise
Austin, Texas
2014

**One Lake's Edge at Hughes
Landing Apartments**
8-Story Mid-rise
The Woodlands, Texas
2015

**Olympia at Willowick
Residences**
8-Story Mid-rise
Houston, Texas
2015

**Gables Cherry Creek Apartments**
8-Story Mid-rise
Denver, Colorado
2016

**Gables Alameda Apartments**
8-Story Mid-rise
Denver, Colorado
2017

**The Katy Apartments**
7-Story Mid-rise
Dallas, Texas
2017

**Preston Hollow Village
Apartments & Retail**
8-Story Mid-rise
Dallas, Texas
2017

**Dinerstein 7th & Grant Apartments**
8-Story Mid-rise
Denver, Colorado
2018

**Hines Sloans Lake Apartments & Retail**
7-Story Mid-rise
Denver, Colorado
2018

**Barryknoll Apartments**
8-Story Mid-rise
Houston, Texas
2018

## OFFICE BUILDINGS

**Imperial Sugar Company**
2-Story Office Building
Sugar Land, Texas
1981

**Sugar Land Telephone Company**
3-Story Office Building
Sugar Land, Texas
1982

**BMC Software Headquarters**
18-Story Office Building
Houston, Texas
1993

**Eldridge Green**
5-Story Office Building
Houston, Texas
2000

**Three Chasewood**
3-Story Office Building
Houston, Texas
2000

**CGG Veritas**
Master Plan and 4 Office Buildings
Houston, Texas
2000-2015

**M.I. Drilling**
5-Story Office Building
Houston, Texas
2004

**Four Chasewood**
4-Story Office Building
Houston, Texas
2004

**BBVA Compass Novo Bank**
18 Branch Bank Locations
Birmingham, Alabama
2011

**Research Forest Lakeside Building Two**
3-Story Office Building
The Woodlands, Texas
2011

**Dress For Success**
2-Story Office Building
Houston, Texas
2012

**Pioneer Natural Resources**
6-Story Office Building
Midland, Texas
2012

**Saudi Consulate**
5-Story Office Building & Residences
The Woodlands, Texas
2013

**Confidential Corporate Campus**
4-Story Corporate Campus
Houston, Texas
2013

**Research Forest Lakeside Building Four**
12-Story Office Building
The Woodlands, Texas
2013

**Research Forest Lakeside Building Five**
8-Story Office Building
The Woodlands, Texas
2014

**San Felipe Place**
17-Story Office Building
Houston, Texas
2015

**Research Forest Lakeside Building Nine**
6-Story Office Building & Retail
The Woodlands, Texas
2015

**Chicago Bridge & Iron**
6-Story Office Building
The Woodlands, Texas
2015

**Westchase Park 2**
6-Story Office Building
Houston, Texas
2015

**Lockton Place**
8-Story Office Building
Houston, Texas
2016

**1111 Travis**
22-Story Office Building
Houston, Texas
2016

**Confidential Office Tower**
23-Story Office Building
Austin, Texas
2018

## MIXED-USE

**G.E. Turtle Creek**
16-Story Office & Hotel
Dallas, Texas
2014

**East Shore**
2-Story Office & Retail
The Woodlands, Texas
2014

**Bridgeland Village Green**
Master Plan & Retail
Cypress, Texas
2016

**Tempe Mixed-Use
Development**
22-Story Office, Apartments,
Grocery & Retail
Tempe, Arizona
2016

**The Perennial**
36-Story Office, Hotel &
Apartments
Houston, Texas
2016

**Alabama Row**
3-Story Office & Retail
Houston, Texas
2017

**Gables Republic Square & Zaza Hotel**
25-Story Apartments & Hotel
Austin, Texas
2017

**Morgan Smith Street**
8-Story Apartments & Grocery
Houston, Texas
2018

**Post Oak Place**
33-Story Office, Apartments, Hotel & Retail
Houston, Texas
2018

**Loews Hotel**
23-Story Hotel
Houston, Texas
2018

**Woodlands Gate**
7-Story Office, Hotel, Entertainment & Retail
Houston, Texas
2018

**Buffalo Heights**
8-Story Apartments, Office,
Grocery & Retail
Houston, Texas
2018

**PMRG Hotel & Residences**
28-Story Tower
Houston, Texas
2019

## WORSHIP

**St. Thomas Aquinas Catholic Church**
College Station, Texas
2004

**Co-Cathedral of the Sacred
Heart**
Houston, Texas
2008

**Northeast Houston Baptist**
Houston, Texas
2008

**Clear Lake United Methodist**
Clear Lake, Texas
2009

**St. Mary's Catholic Church**
Plantersville, Texas
2010

**Memorial Lutheran**
Houston, Texas
2010

**Lakewood United Methodist**
Houston, Texas
2010

**Christ Church United Methodist**
The Woodlands, Texas
2011

**St. John Lutheran**
Cypress, Texas
2011

**First Baptist Church
Pasadena**
Pasadena, Texas
2012

**Universal Church Westpark**
Houston, Texas
2012

**Atascocita United Methodist Church**
Humble, Texas
2013

**Christ Community Church**
Houston, Texas
2014

**Kingwood United Methodist**
Kingwood, Texas
2015

**Austin Chinese Church**
Austin, Texas
2016

**Sacred Heart Catholic Church**
Conroe, Texas
2016

## EDUCATION

**Houston Child Guidance Center**
Houston, Texas
1985

**Wesley Elementary**
New Library & Classroom Building
Houston, Texas
1989

**The Kinkaid School**
Lower School
Houston, Texas
2000

**University of St. Thomas**
Humanities/Education Building
Houston, Texas
2001

**The Kinkaid School**
Center for Student Life, Fine Arts
& Administration
Houston, Texas
2004

**St. John School**
Master Plan, Renovation & New
Classroom Buildings
Houston, Texas
2007

**Pope John XXIII High School**
Master Plan & Gymnasium
Katy, Texas
2008

**St. Agnes Academy**
Athletic Complex
Houston, Texas
2010

**St. Rose of Lima Catholic School**
Campus Expansion
Houston, Texas
2012

**First Baptist Christian Academy**
New Construction
Pasadena, Texas
2014

**Pope John XXIII High School**
Student Center
Katy, Texas
2015

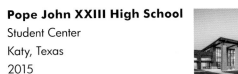

**The Village School**
Finna Center & New Middle School
Houston, Texas
2015

**The John Cooper School**
Rock, Math & Science Center
The Woodlands, Texas
2016

**Episcopal High School**
Master Plan & Student Center
Houston, Texas
2017

**Covenant Preparatory School**
Master Plan & New Construction
Kingwood, Texas
2018

## INTERIOR DESIGN

**NASA Visitors Center**
Houston, Texas
1988

**Credit Suisse**
Houston, Texas
1989

**Banque Paribas**
Houston, Texas
1991

**McKinsey & Company**
Dallas, Texas
1990

**Credit Suisse**
Miami, Florida
1991

**Torch Energy**
Houston, Texas
1991

**TEPPCO**
Houston, Texas
1992

**Kent Electronics**
Houston, Texas
1992

**BMC Software**
Houston, Texas
1992

**Space Industries**
Washington, DC
1993

**DHL Airways, Inc.**
Houston, Texas
1994

**Houston Industries**
Houston, Texas
1994

**DHL Airways, Inc.**
Houston, Texas
1994

**Johnson & Higgins**
Houston, Texas
1995

**Haynes & Boone**
Houston, Texas
1995

**Santa Fe Energy**
Houston, Texas
1995

**Ikon Office Solutions**
Houston, Texas
1996

**Winstead Sechrest**
Houston, Texas
1997

**Edge Petroleum**
Houston, Texas
1997

**Tejas Gas Corporation**
Houston, Texas
1998

**Amerada Hess Corporation**
Houston, Texas
1998

**Andersen Consulting**
Houston, Texas
1998

**Savage Design**
Houston, Texas
1999

**Bellwether Exploration**
Houston, Texas
1999

**Alto Technologies Resources**
Houston, Texas
2000

**Sapient**
Houston, Texas
2000

**Devon Energy**
Houston, Texas
2001

**Parker Drilling**
Houston, Texas
2001

**Devon Energy**
Houston, Texas
2001

**Shell Trading**
Houston, Texas
2002

**Alley Theatre**
Houston, Texas
1996

**Strasburger & Price**
Houston, Texas
2002

**Thompson, Knight, Brown, Parker & Leahy**
Houston, Texas
2002

**Noble Energy**
Houston, Texas
2002

**KPMG**
San Francisco, California
2004

**Chamberlain Hrdlicka**
Houston, Texas
2004

**Texas Genco**
Houston, Texas
2005

**Hein & Associates**
Houston, Texas
2005

**Enterprise Products**
Houston, Texas
2006

**Wachovia Houston Office**
Houston, Texas
2006

**Pride International - Lv. 45**
Houston, Texas
2007

**Barclays Capital**
Houston, Texas
2007

**Hess**
Houston, Texas
2007

**Det Norske Veritas**
Houston, Texas
2008

**CBRE/Trammell Crow**
Houston, Texas
2008

**Veritas**
Houston, Texas
2008

**Morgan, Lewis & Bockius**
Houston, Texas
2008

**KPMG**
Dallas, Texas
2008

**Parker Drilling - Relocation**
Houston, Texas
2008

**Veritas**
Houston, Texas
2009

**Weatherford**
Houston, Texas
2010

**Apache Corporation**
Midland, Texas
2010

**Schlumberger Financial Hub**
Houston, Texas
2011

**Lloyd's Register Americas**
Houston, Texas
2011

**Briggs & Veselka Co.**
Houston, Texas
2011

**Schlumberger Operations Center**
Houston, Texas
2011

**Nexeo Solutions**
Houston, Texas
2012

**Pioneer Natural Resources**
Houston, Texas
2012

**Helix Energy Solutions**
Houston, Texas
2012

**Rosetta Resources**
Houston, Texas
2012

**Apache Corporation - Three Post Oak**
Houston, Texas
2012

**Noble Drilling - Training Facility**
Houston, Texas
2012

**Crown Castle**
Houston, Texas
2013

**Ziegler Cooper Architects**
Houston, Texas
2013

**Chicago Bridge & Iron Corporate Campus**
The Woodlands, Texas
2013

**Memorial Resources**
Houston, Texas
2014

**Repsol Services Co.**
The Woodlands, Texas
2014

**Coats Rose**
Houston, Texas
2014

**Alliantgroup**
Houston, Texas
2014

**Apache Corporation Lobby**
Houston, Texas
2014

**Apache Corporation - Cafe & Fitness**
Houston, Texas
2015

**Post Oak Commons**
Houston, Texas
2015

**Datacert, Inc.**
Houston, Texas
2015

**Skanska Houston Office**
Houston, Texas
2015

**Veterans Evaluation Services**
Houston, Texas
2015

**Zachry Group**
Houston, Texas
2015

**Stoller Group**
Houston, Texas
2016

**Parkway Properties**
Houston, Texas
2016

**Newmark Grubb Knight Frank**
Houston, Texas
2016

**W.D. Von Gonten**
Houston, Texas
2016

**JPMorgan Chase Client Conference Center**
Houston, Texas
2016

**JPMorgan Chase Strategic Hub**
Houston, Texas
2016

**G&A Partners**
Houston, Texas
2016

**DesignHive**
Houston, Texas
2017

**COMMERCIAL REDEVELOPMENT**

**2000 West Loop South**
Houston, Texas
1990

**Allen Center**
Houston, Texas
1994

**Houston Industries Headquarters**
Houston, Texas
1996

**Louisiana Place**
Houston, Texas
1996

**America Tower**
Houston, Texas
1999

**777 Post Oak**
Houston, Texas
1999

**2200 West Loop South**
Houston, Texas
2000

**Brookhollow Central**
Houston, Texas
2006

**801 Travis**
Houston, Texas
2007

**Post Oak Central**
Houston, Texas
2008

**801 Louisiana**
Houston, Texas
2008

**1300 Main**
Houston, Texas
2009

**3355 West Alabama**
Houston, Texas
2009

**5 Greenway Plaza**
Houston, Texas
2010

**20555 SH 249**
Houston, Texas
2011

**11 Greenway Plaza**
Houston, Texas
2011

**515 Post Oak**
Houston, Texas
2011

**One City Centre**
Houston, Texas
2011

**5444 Westheimer**
Houston, Texas
2012

**Brookhollow One**
Houston, Texas
2013

**2000 St. James**
Houston, Texas
2013

**Park Laureate**
Houston, Texas
2014

**3040 Post Oak**
Houston, Texas
2015

**20 Greenway Plaza**
Houston, Texas
2015

**Four Oaks**
Houston, Texas
2016

**3 Greenway Plaza**
Houston, Texas
2016

**Greenway Plaza - Food
Court & Fitness**
Houston, Texas
2016

**San Felipe Plaza**
Houston, Texas
2016

**Park Towers**
Houston, Texas
2016

**8 Greenway Plaza**
Houston, Texas
2017

**800 Bell**
Houston, Texas
2017

**9 Greenway Plaza**
Houston, Texas
2017

**12 Greenway Plaza**
Houston, Texas
2017

# ACKNOWLEDGMENTS

Ziegler Cooper would like to express our deepest gratitude and appreciation to all of our colleagues at the firm, both past and present, for their continued dedication and faithful pursuit of design excellence. Of equal importance, we thank our clients and friends for their ongoing support, which has been vital to the success of the firm. As we look to our future, we feel comforted to know that we have a talented team in place to carry forward the proud legacy of our past forty years.

## FOUNDING PRINCIPALS

Scott Ziegler, AIA; Senior Principal, Urban Residential Studio
Michael Cooper, AIA

## CURRENT SHAREHOLDERS

Mark Nolen, AIA, LEED AP; Senior Principal, Workplace Interiors Studio
Kurt Hull, AIA, LEED AP; Senior Principal, Corporate & Commercial Architecture Studio
Jim Zemski, AIA; Managing Principal, Urban Residential Studio
Rafael Feinstein, RA; Principal, Urban Residential Studio
Amy Jochem, IIDA, LEED AP; Principal, Workplace Interiors Studio
Steve Lucchesi, AIA; Principal, Community Architecture Studio
Chris Petrash, AIA; Principal, Urban Residential Studio
Denny Simon, AIA; Principal, Urban Residential Studio
Paul Wilkinson, IIDA, TAID, LEED AP; Principal, Workplace Interiors Studio
Maria Aquino, IIDA, TAID; Associate Principal, Workplace Interiors Studio
Wimberly Barra, IIDA, LLED AP; Associate Principal, Workplace Interiors Studio
Susan Dieterich, AIA, LEED AP; Associate Principal, Community Architecture Studio

Liz Friedman, IIDA, LEED AP; Associate Principal, Workplace Interiors Studio
Leanna Gatlin, AIA, LEED AP BD+C; Associate Principal, Corporate & Commercial Architecture Studio
Dawna Houchin, AIA, LEED AP; Associate Principal, Urban Residential Studio
Michelle Kerstein, IIDA; Associate Principal, Workplace Interiors Studio
Eric Korth, AIA; Associate Principal, Community Architecture Studio
Charles Middlebrooks, AIA, CSI, LEED AP EB+OM; Associate Principal, Urban Residential Studio
Sandra Morrison, RA, LEED AP; Associate Principal, Urban Residential Studio
Manuel Navarro, RID; Associate Principal, Workplace Interiors Studio
Karene Smithhart; Associate Principal, Controller
Axel Weisheit, AIA; Associate Principal, Urban Residential Studio
Bin Yu, AIA, LEED AP; Associate Principal, Corporate & Commercial Architecture Studio

# PHOTOGRAPHY CREDITS

Joe Aker:
1111 Travis, The Broadway, Chicago Bridge & Iron, Co-Cathedral of the Sacred Heart, Dress For Success, The Kinkaid School, Parker Drilling, Repsol, Research Forest Lakeside 2, Research Forest Lakeside 4 & 5, San Felipe Place, St. John School, TEPPCO, Villa d'Este & Montebello

Mabry Campbell:
Four Oaks, Skanska, The Village School

George Craig:
Highland Tower

Jud Haggard:
3 Greenway, 2727 Kirby, Atascocita United Methodist Church, First Baptist Pasadena, Memorial Lutheran Church, Pope John XXIII High School, The Sapphire, St. John Lutheran, Universal Church Westpark, Westchase Park II, Ziegler Cooper Architects

Paul Hester:
Four Chasewood, Highland Tower

Ben Hill:
Gables River Oaks, Gables Tanglewood, Olympia at Willowick, One Lake's Edge, The Sovereign

Ed LaCasse:
Hanover Southampton

David Lauer:
Gables Cherry Creek

John C. Lindy:
St. Mary's Plantersville

Yang Liu:
Dust Jacket & Section Pages

Thomas McConnell:
The Austonian

Peter Molick:
DesignHive, G&A Partners, Hanover Southampton, Parkway Properties, Pope John XXIII High School, Stoller Group, W.D. Von Gonten

Chas Schreiber:
Gables Park Plaza Tower

Gary Zvonkovic:
20 Greenway, Alliantgroup, Apache Café & Fitness, CGG, Christ Church United Methodist, Datacert, Kingwood United Methodist Church, Post Oak Commons, St. Rose of Lima Catholic School

.index

Published by:
Visual Profile Books, Inc.
389 Fifth Avenue, New York, NY 10016
Phone: 212.279.7000
www.visualprofilebooks.com

Distributed by:
National Book Networks, Inc.
15200 NBN Way, Blue Ridge Summit, PA 17214
Toll Free (U.S.): 800.462.6420
Toll Free Fax (U.S.): 800.338.4550
Email orders or Inquires: customercare@nbnbooks.com

Library of Congress Cataloging in Publication Data:
Ziegler Cooper: 40 Years of Inspirational Design

ISBN 13: 978-0-9975489-5-2
ISBN 10: 0-9975489-5-9

HAISSAM ABDUL-KADER · JILL ALEXANDER · JABIR AL-HILALI · RICHIE ALIGO · GILFORD ALLEN · MARK ALLEN · YOELKI AMADOR · GRACIE
DEBRA BACH · CATHERINE BADGER · NICHOLAS BAKAYSA · SAMEER BALVALLY · CHRIS BARBOZA · CLAIBORNE BARKER · ASHLEY BA
JACKIE BATSON · MARTHA BAUMAN · CATHERINE BEATHARD · KATE BEHELFER · JAMES BELLAMY · JOHN BELLIAN · VIKKI BENEFIEL · G
KAREN BISCHOF · ELENOR BISSELL · CASEY BISWELL · LAURIE BISWELL · MARY BLAKENEY · CODY BLANCHARD · JASZMINE BOLDEN
ANN BUFORD · TOAN BUI · JILL BURDISS · BARBARA BURKHARDT · BILL BURWELL · JACK CADE · SCOTT CALLAWAY · JOSHUA CALUAG
SUE COLE · KRISTEN COLLINS-NOLEN · JANE COMINSKY · MICHAEL COOPER · GEORGE COVACEVICH · LAURA CRAGLE · BENJAMIN
DANIEL DAVIS · JANE DAVIS · ROSS DAVIS · SARAH DE ITA · CYNTHIA DENNIS · STACEY DEPEW · MYRA DEYHLE · JENNIFER DIDA
JOHN DOODY · ERIN DOREY · MARGARET DOUGLASS · JENNIFER DOYLE · KEVIN DUESTERHOFT · VANESSA DUHON · CARI DU
KATHLEEN ENGLISH · TIFFANI EPPERSON-REEVE · DAVID EPSTEIN · JOSE ESCUDERO · NICOLE ESTES · CHRIS EVERS · KATHLEEN FABIANI
CAREY FREGIA · ASHLEY FRIDELL · ELIZABETH FRIEDMAN · CORINNA FRITSCH · LUKE FRY · MARIA FUENTES · MEGAN FUNNI · DANKA
ZAKI GHANEM · MARCIA GIBSON · JAMES GILFORD · AMY GILMORE · JAMES GLASSMAN · CAROLYN GLENN · CEDRA GOLDMA
RYAN GORDON · JULIA GRAY · HEATHER GRIFFIN · SCOTT GRIFFITH · ISRAEL GRINBERG · VIVIAN GUAN · DAVID GUERRERO · MARR
AUDREY HARDESTY · ROBERT HARDY · LAUREN HARPER · KAREN HARRIS · AMY HASSELL · BOSHA HASZLAKIEWICZ-KUAN · TERESA HAV
DENISE HERRERA · MARIBETH HERRINGTON · KATHERINE HESS · JOHN HETTWER · MERRIE HEVRDEJS · DONALD HICKEY · MICKIE HILL · A
DAWNA HOUCHIN · CHRISTINA HOXIE · KURT HULL · MCKENZIE HULL · ALLYSON HUTCHINSON · DAVID ICKES · JAMES IRVINE · JO
COURTNEY JOHNSON · DEAN JOHNSON · GRACE JOHNSON · WARREN JOHNSON · ALEXANDRA JOO · MELANIE JOSEPH · PETER
HYDER KAZIM · GEORGE KEES · RON KELLER · PAMELA KELLEY · GWENDOLYN KELLY · MICHELLE KERSTEIN · ROXIE KEY · MEGAN
KENT KOSCHANY · MICHELLE KOUDSI · LINDSEY KOWALKOWSKI · FRANK KRENEK · JUDITH KUGLE · DONA KURYANOWICZ · ALISO
HENG-HUI LEE · WENDY LEE · JOHN LEMR · MICHELLE LESTER · CHRISTINA LETOURNEAU · ROY LEWIS · MICHELLE LIM · DIANA LIN
STEPHEN LUCCHESI · LAUREY LUCREE · ED LUI · HAI LUU · REBECCA LYONS · KELLY LYONS-PAVLAT · ALICE MACFARLANE · LAURA MANCH
BRADLY MCCARROLL · MICHELE MCCUTCHEN · CYNTHIA MCDANIEL · JIM MCDANIELL · LAUREN MCDERMOTT · BOBBY MCGHEE · SAM
CHARLES MIDDLEBROOKS · KELLEY MILLER · MARCIA MINK · JEAN MINKLER · YANCEY MODESTO · ANDREA MOEDER · THEODORE MO
DOROTHY MOROZ · TRACY MORRISON · SANDRA MORRISON · CARL MULLINS · JULIAN MUNOZ · ILIANA MURPHY · LAURA NAGALA · A
DOAN NGUYENDAM · MARK NOLEN · ROBERT NOLEN · ENES OKIC · PAIGE OLIVE · DONOVAN OLLIFF · GABRIEL OLMOS · AMY C
ALLISON PARROTT · TAMMY PARSONS · MICHAEL PATAMAT · NEETA PATEL · TAMI PEARSON · MICHAEL PENNINGTON · CHRISTINA
JENNIFER POWELL · LAURA PRATER · JUTTA PRESENTI · FANI QANO · FRED QUINTERO · ANDREA RAFIEI · TATE RAGLAND · KAREN RAN
LYNETTE RHEW · RICHARD RIVERA · JOHN RIVERS · BRUCE ROADCAP · CHRIS ROBERTS · RACHEL ROBERTS · RICHARD RODGERS · JUAN RO
MIKE RUEZ · JULIE RUFFINO · STEPHEN RUIZ · XIOMARA RUIZ · CATHERINE RUNNER · DONNY RUSSELL · LARISA RYZHIK · SIMON SA
LESLEY SCHMIDT · SYLVAN SCHURWANZ · BILLYE SCOTT · DANIEL SEARIGHT · HAIG SELIAN · CAROLINE SERNA · ELENA SEVASTIANI · I
CHRISTY SHOOP · STEVEN SHWARTZ · CARLOS SIERRA · DENNY SIMON · JACKIE SIMPSON · VERONICA SIMPSON · LOUIS SKIDMO
ROBERT SMITHHART · DEREK SOLTES · ROGER SOTO · ERIN SOZA · PAULA SPELLMAN · REBECCA SPURGEON · JENNA STANKE · G
MELISSA TAYLOR · RALPH TAYLOR · AMANDA TEETER · BREIT TERPELUK · BERT TIBBITS · THOMAS TIEN · MICHAEL TOPPING · JESSICA
MICHAEL VALENZUELA · JOANN VALLIE-RUSH · RICK VANETTEN · PAULETTE VARNER · SHEILA VAUGHN · BETZA VEGA-SMITH · MARK
DANIEL WALLACE · KATHARINE WATSON · JAMES WAY · ELIZABETH WEATHERS · RONALD WEDEMEYER · AXEL WEISHEIT · JACKIE WELLS
KELLY WILLIAMSON · RYAN WILSON · SHANE WILSON · MICHAEL WINDLE · MICHAEL WINGATE · LAUREN WINTERBAUER · NEDWAN
KAYVAN ZAREA · MATTHEW ZAWACKI · JALAL ZEITOLINE · JOSHUA ZELLER · PETER ZELLER · JAMES ZELISKI